Amy Bornman's poems pie[...] are what I wanted to read [...] baby. Even now they provide me a balm and poetic [...] dialogue between the self, with the mysterious body and soul that dwells in the womb, and a cloud of biblical women who have journeyed through the blood and beauty of motherhood. **These poems peel back and reveal the glory and terror, the sacred and mundane, a mother's cry and prayer.** *Broken Waters* is a kind of examination of conscience and a blessing.

JESS SWEENEY
cofounder of Wellspring: A Mother Artist Project and director of
the Collegium Institute's Arts Initiative

Penned during the COVID-19 pandemic, Bornman's poetry exudes a wisdom drawn from introspection and solitude that is reminiscent of Emily Dickinson's. Bornman's poetry reveals what readers of scripture should have seen all along: motherhood is central to the biblical narrative. She draws upon Biblical imagery—water and fire, bleeding and cleansing, birth and crucifixion—to audaciously poeticize her own experience as a mother through her pregnancy, labor, and the birth of her first child. By narrating her own maternal experiences alongside those of biblical mothers, Bornman invites the reader to experience a sacred history of motherhood. To read these poems is to intimately experience the mind and body of a mother: beginning and ending, inside and outside, birthing and dying. After reading this collection, I feel even more fully that scripture is for me, is about me, as a woman, a child, and a mother.

ALISON GIBSON
Senior Lecturer of English and Director of First-Year Writing and
the Writing Center at Wheaton College

My oldest was born over eleven years ago, but Amy Bornman brought back the exquisitely excruciating details of those months of pregnancy with this beautiful book of poetry. From the days of longing for a pregnancy ("I think I want to be transformed") to the delivery room ("my body/ will be broken and your body/ will be whole and we'll go out/ together to see what remains") Amy walks through each week of pregnancy ("I've never kept time in weeks before") with such care and intention ("you are a fact in me"). Interspersed are searing views of biblical women like Leah ("I think/ they're the best children/ in this terrible world") and Noah's wife (*"why am I on this ark?"*) written as you've never read them before. As a reader, you will remember your own experiences or perhaps gain a clearer glimpse of what your friend, your partner, your family has felt in these isolating months of transformation. "I will die in a thousand tiny ways, having met you/ on earth where we don't know anything." This book is the diary I didn't keep during my own pregnancies, and I am grateful to have read it.

JOANN RENEE BOSWELL
author of *Meta-Verse!: it's going to be interesting to see how yesterday goes*
(Fernwood Press, 2023)

Broken Waters

poems

amy bornman

Fernwood
PRESS

Broken Waters

Printed in the United States of America

Page design: Mareesa Fawver Moss
Cover art: Claire Waterman

ISBN 978-1-59498-125-8

for Thomas—little doubt, little fish, little bird

Contents

Introduction

Before becoming pregnant, I carried around with me for years
what might have been my most helpful self-reflective thought—
when I have children, my life will change forever. I knew this, and not only
knew it, but *knew* it. Shortly before my husband and I began to
"try," I remember writing this cynical but deeply honest poem
in my journal—so honest that I never shared it with anyone,
until now:

> I'd like to have a baby because I'd like to
> ruin my life. I fear death, so I'll create
> tiny beloved creatures and fear death
> even more. I have an artistic interest
> in motherhood which might make me
> an intrinsically unfit mother before I
> even begin. It feels like a puzzle I have
> no right to be working on, yet here I am,
> midnight, at the table gathering edge
> pieces. I've always felt this way though.
> The little death a woman dies is the
> most compelling thing in the world.

Somehow I could sense this particular transformation
coming for me. For years. I thought about motherhood long
before I was pregnant, more than anyone really ought to. I

think I could also sense a sort of calling in motherhood, a magnetic pull in that direction, almost against my will. It scared me more than anything else. This was my angel to wrestle all through the night, no telling what I'd find in the morning. *I won't let you go unless you bless me.*

You could call this book an extended meditation on a text, the text being motherhood as explored through stories of women and motherhood in the Bible and through my own first experience of pregnancy, birth, and early postpartum. Being pregnant felt like a slow freefall into an unknown ocean. A really slow freefall, nine whole months. Such a vivid embodiment of the oft-repeated Christian saying, "Now but not yet." My husband and I even got into arguments a few times about whether or not I was a mother yet when I was pregnant. I wanted to say that I was, but I knew it wasn't quite true. I was but I wasn't. It was complete and also completely incomplete. Using that time to write about what was changing in me and to, like a detective, investigate where I could see echoes of motherhood in the text of the Bible, felt like one of the only ways to work out my wrestling, an action I could carry out in the mostly inactive waiting experience of pregnancy.

Though we were actively hoping to start our family, when I became pregnant, I was terrified. *This is it*, I thought. *The beginning of the end*. I couldn't wait to meet our child; I was so curious and hopeful but also full of grief, full of fear. Transformation is painful. Every mother I knew, especially my friends who were new mothers too, just ahead of me, expressed a rawness, a tension, a beautiful, difficult change in motherhood that they knew they'd spend the rest of their life trying to reconcile. My life, my body, my self as I'd always known it was so slowly being pulled out from under me. I knew that becoming a parent would have to first tear me in two. They don't tell you about what Adrienne Rich calls "the psychic crisis of bearing a first child." They don't tell you that you will lose much of what you think you should be holding onto, that there's a sort of death that accompanies the birth.

These poems are about pregnancy and birth, but they're also just as much about faith and practice, about God. Amongst all the other changes, throughout my pregnancy, I found myself markedly unable to pray or even to really *think* about God in any way that felt familiar to me. I also found myself unable to read the Bible like I had before, turning to books and writings about motherhood and pregnancy instead, seeking women's stories and voices and quiet domestic wisdom, hearing this almost as something that sounds awfully like the voice of God I've heard in the past—that recognition, truth like a flame. When I did turn to the text of the Bible, it was to find the women in it. I was reading mothers (who are more sparse than they should be). The mothers in the Bible do desperate things, remarkable things—what more would we learn if we got to spend more time with them? What if all this were a matriarchy? And maybe it kind of is? Maybe God is as much a mother as a father? I would argue that the text supports this idea, though it could be seen as absurd or heresy to some. That wondering, that hunch, that growing stormy rage that we don't speak of such things in every church everywhere is the origin of many of the poems in this collection.

I learned as vividly as possible that becoming a parent is a conversion and a dramatic one at that. I'm not sure that anything more earth-shattering, angel-in-your-bedroom, road-to-Damascus, burning-bush-esque has ever happened to me. Where else to turn but the place where all these somewhat wild stories converge and get spun into meaning? The Bible became a better *What to Expect When You're Expecting* than any book I read about birth (of which I read many). When your child is born, through blood, sweat, screams, pain, you are born again. It's a window into the suffering of Christ; it's an invitation into profound sacrifice, maybe one of the clearest and most ordinary forms on earth. I suppose there's a reason that the Bible uses birth as a metaphor over and over—all creation groaning in labor. It's how we all got here, after all. Not one of us is spared from that origin story. Even if we don't remember being born, we were. And I will never in my life be able to forget giving birth.

In becoming a mother, I kept meeting Jesus—maybe for the first time, honestly. Meeting Jesus in inky midnight, waiting in the garden. Meeting Jesus on the cross as I endured contractions in unmedicated labor. Hearing his motherhood in the way he spoke to his friends, telling simple stories, gentle instructions, his disciples like children. Jesus' healing touch, the gift of his attention, his gentleness and rage, his enduring patience, his fierce need for solitude, his sensitivity to the softest touch. I began to recognize that, all along, Jesus was the perfect image of both the mother and the child, the nurturer and the one to be nurtured in me. Like caring for the stranger on the road, what I do for my baby, I do for Jesus. Shortly after my son, Thomas, was born, I had a stark moment of recognition, changing his diaper, bone tired: *This is Christ*.

I first learned I was pregnant in a pandemic Lent. My son was born in Advent. And now, as I complete this introduction, years have passed, and it will soon be Lent again. I feel a sort of circumference, a return to the start of the circle. I'm in the throes of motherhood now and pregnant for the second time, the deep tide of change pulling me in and out. I've lived some of the greatest intensity of love and pain I could ever have imagined in mothering my first child, preparing for another, and I know, now more than ever, that there's so much more to come. I can see that I was right to spend all those years bracing for motherhood, anticipating it with fear and trembling, but I can also now sing of a sweetness that is far past what I imagined. Having met my child, so hoped for and imagined, I feel sort of drained of poetry. The words come slowly now. I'm not so sure what to say—and I'm surprised by how clearly the words came as I waited to give birth, how much I already knew. And isn't that sort of wonderfully fitting? That now, for a little while, seeing my son grow day by day and feeling a new mystery soul growing in my body is all the poetry, all the prayer, all the creation I need?

Baby boy "Thomas" born on 12/3/20 @ 0538 @ 40w1d.
Apgars 8/9. Wt: 7#10oz
Uncomplicated pregnancy, spontaneous labor, normal vaginal birth.
"Amy labored with grace."

—from the midwife's report

Eden

you are in eden now.
you will fall, be pushed out,
eat the fruit of the living
that I hold in my outstretched palm.
do you want to become wise?
do you want to wander through
the wilderness? I weep as I hand
it to you. I am snake and tree at once.
and I am your mother, sending you away
with flaming swords blocking the
garden gate, but always listening
for your cries in the dark.

Ash Wednesday

it rains steadily all afternoon
on into evening on ash wednesday,
and I am not pregnant. I bleed instead,
bright crimson, rust, black, an egg
in me turns to dust, something never lived.
it's terribly ordinary, common,
as steady month by month as
the moon since I was twelve,
but now I feel the child I dared to imagine ask me,
"where is your god?" and I can't answer.

add the ashes to my forehead
as something is taken away.
I decrease and think of my womb
and its own unknowing, its holy detachment,
dealing with death like routine,
taking care of itself by sweeping the crumbs
from under the table, a meditation—
I didn't expect to feel such keen desire.

and no way to know how many months,
years, it will take. I feel slippery, guilty
sadness, having only just begun to hope,
having not even lost anything yet,
not really. I know women who can't conceive,
and my own mother's multiple miscarriages,
remember her telling me about them
in detail over italian food long ago.

earlier today I walked the dog and touched
my gut thinking, *empty*.
everyone here can hear the rain on the roof.
yet even now, says the lord, return to me.
I do, or I mean to. I buy a pregnancy test
at target for next month's try.
who knows whether god will turn
and leave a blessing. so I'll turn, I will,
between now and the end of time,
though I know nothing of what it is I ask for.
I think I want to be transformed.

God

not my beginning but yours.
I was hovering over new waters,
fluttering, trembling, crouching
to give birth. I am an eagle over
her nest. I am wind over the hard
shape of earth. I am moon pulling
tide, dividing self from self,
I make all these things in the image
of myself and then I make you,
breaking darkness in two
for first light.

Five Weeks

I sit in the kitchen while the priest strips
the altar, and the lights go out slowly
in a nave across the locked-down city.

the back door swings open and shut on its own,
a great gust with wind chimes—
wild—rain, and hail. which plague is this?

it still moves me even though it's all on a screen,
livestream. I'm rapt, though the dog barks,
and I'm at home, everything different this triduum.

my nausea, fatigue, my too-much-to-lose,
my bread, my wine, my unwashed feet,
passover lamb the size of a pea,
I sit in an upper room up forty red stairs
in my house on a night full of wind.

Eve

of every woman I am first. imagine
me falling off a cliff. imagine me drowning
in the tide. my belly growing big, for what?
no one can tell me what's going on.
nausea I don't understand, weeping for
hormones with no name. prayer with
no answer, when before I looked up
and everything was there. desert
instead of garden, a green twig bending,
bending, never snapping, and I am in
labor forever. no midwife, no mother,
no sister, no friend. I say goodbye to everything
because I'm sure that I will die. this is mine
alone. I remember the curse, it made no sense.
no knowledge could prepare me for this.
it is not pain, it's the end of the world. I walk
through it, screaming, to find somewhere new.

Six Weeks

I'll hold you loosely. you may die.
I want you, and I don't. I'm not
sure who you'll be or if you'll live
any longer than these few weeks
when I mostly didn't know about
you and these last days when I've been
tired and sick, getting nothing done.
it feels nice to have something to blame,
especially something as sweet as a
very small group of cells. I listen to poets
read poems in new york city that aren't
about babies, and I wonder about
wanting you. does it make me
too soft? around the middle, but also
my heart? I can only write my poems,
and I can only bear my child.
it will be different for me than for anyone else.
saying that out loud sounds petty
or selfish. isn't this my chance to brush
up against something universal and infinite?
to become a part of the world?
before you're a mother, you can be
somewhat undetectable. no longer.
you are the size of a sweet pea,
and I am the size of a woman.
I'll carry you as long as you're
small enough. then, I guess,
my arms will get stronger.

Noah's Wife

on the boat watching the rooftops
slowly sink, drenched children standing on top
with their mothers who are weeping.

she thinks of each of her babies drowning,
sees it in her mind. her babies, now grown,
strong and able to swim.

are you sure? she turns and looks noah in the eye.
she's desperate now, wants to grab the nearest
tree limb. *why am I on this ark?*

Eight Weeks

have I failed you already,
my dragonfly with the newest wings?
I have, and I'll fail you many more times,
over and over, until it's a grief between us
that is also a joy, or at least a sort of truth.
make me more honest. make me less sure.
I already feel myself change like my skin
is peeling, and I can't stop it falling.
is it my work to protect you?
or to imagine that I could, to suspend
my disbelief, to hope on your behalf
as long as we live? we never had control.
you will grow however you will,
despite my best efforts, and I will carry you
imperfectly. but maybe I'll be christ to you,
when my small self subsides sometimes.
maybe the truth will reach through me
when we least expect it, and you'll be blessed.
that would be good. that would be the best thing
that could happen to us both. give us the benediction
both of us deserve but can't muster on purpose,
on our own.

Lot's Wife

salt woman has worried a lot, lived
somewhere terrible, tried her best
and still did poorly.
salt woman is a mother,
salt woman had friends in that city.
salt woman looked back.

salt woman is salty. salt woman
double-checks, indulges, is willful.
salt woman has control of her head.
salt woman did everything she could,

gave her body as a pillar,
here, let me hold you up,
with all of my sorrows
I season your sea.

Nine Weeks

you're more in my body than in my mind.
I can hardly imagine you, hardly think
beyond some vacant fear that you'll
never arrive. you are silent and tiny,
the only evidence my total lack of
appetite for anything but cheese pizzas
from all over town and plain greek yogurt
each morning first thing, my tiredness
like weights on each limb. sometimes
I worry that I dreamed the whole thing,
and I'll have to explain that you never
were at all. but that's just worry,
you are a fact in me.

soon I will burst forward with belly
and kicks to the weight of you,
the realness of your life beginning.
but now you are nothing but a faint thought
and discomfort. I'm sorry to call you nothing.
after this, you'll never be nothing again.

Sarah

after I am completely dried out
will there be yet for me wetness?
will there be sudden burst of
passion—a laugh like a moan?

have I been too woman for you?
after years of sitting silently in
my longing, standing on the edge
of hope—I have wanted to hold

you in my arms. I have wanted to
do something private and good.
I give myself away by my joy.
I give myself away every day.

Ten Weeks

you will always be my mystery, my
undoing, the one who will rip me in two.
I will know you as I know myself, a sort of
unknowing, where I see best when I
squint, when I blink, when I sleep.
my first baby, where have you been?
oh egg I've carried since the day I was born,
will you now blossom so I can see?
what will you do to me? you are mystical
and actual, you are human and soul.
this year has brought so many hopes to me,
and now I stand under them like a canopy
and weep.

Shiphrah and Puah

you lie to the king and his men,
all of them uncomfortable in your
presence, the smell of you, amniotic
and iron-y, your tied-back hair, your
layers of clothing, the wild look in your
eyes betraying the things you've seen.
they believe you because they know
nothing of birth, no notion of where
they came from, of what women know,
the deep waters. you tell them the
hebrew women birthed boy after boy
without your help. not true, for your very
hands were the ones that caught them
beneath the birthing stool, the ones that
lifted them up to the terrified mothers.
you lift up these hands in innocence now,
in the king's spotless throne room.
they can't see that you're in the middle of a
long and painful labor, your face not twisted
anymore when the pain comes, too late
for that. they don't know that you'll do anything
to make way for this newness, that you're thinking
about dying even now. and they do not notice
the waters bursting and parting,
running right through the middle of you.

Twelve Weeks

I heard your heart beat for the first time,
deep in the sea of my body.
the midwife moved the wand
across my skin, and it took so long
to find you that I worried you
couldn't be found. I didn't hear
anything I recognized, just shipwreck
and whale song. where are you swimming
with small quick strokes and
water breaths? the midwife said,
"there it is," and at first I didn't hear.
the smallest sound, your body alive.
I heard your heart, fast, and just barely.
there you are in me, little fish.
deeper than anywhere I've ever been.

afterward I bought two slices of pizza
and ate them standing in the kitchen.
one day I'll buy pizza slices for you
while we wait for the end of time.

Moses

how could I send you in a
basket down the river without
crawling into the basket too?
peeling you from my breast like
tearing out my organs, and each
morning I'll wake up yelling
your name into the orange dawn,
making clouds from the heat of
my breath. I'll drown in your place,
die at the top of the hill,
and you'll float away from me
to your whole life.

Thirteen Weeks

the dog woke me up in the
middle of the night crying
at the back door to go out.
as I waited for him, I thought
this will be us. how many
middle-nights will we see?

The Plagues

1.

the river became blood,
and the dust became gnats,
and the frogs got into everything,
the kitchens, the beds.
it's not a way to live,
to see your home infested
with strange creatures in
great numbers, sent by
some foreign god. the mothers
just trying to feed children,
the nauseous pregnant women
weeping at frogs in bowls,
wiping gnats out of babies'
eyes, going for the water and
finding blood instead.
it's not a way to live, on
an earth beset with plagues.
it seems one leaves, and the
next one comes. isn't this
already hard enough?

2.

there were flies everywhere,
then all the animals died
in the fields. boils on everyone's
skin, then hail that came
with fire. all the trees were gone.
then locusts to eat what was left
(and what was?), followed by
three full days of the deepest darkness,
so no one left their houses.
but they hadn't wanted to
for days anyway, people walking
like ghosts through the streets
wearing black, skin peeling,
swatting bugs away, dodging dead
animals like some terrible dream.
everywhere grief and nowhere to go.

but the worst thing was a rumor
that spread, a whisper of
one more terror, unspeakable,
women staring at sons,
watching them breathe
through the night,
lighting precious candles in
the darkness, please stay alive,
if I keep watch maybe
I can undo all of this.

3.

and there was a great cry in egypt,
for there was not a house where
someone was not dead. up and
down every alley, every sidewalk,
through every open window,
the sound of weeping. they carried their
dead out of their houses, their precious
boys, some only just born. they looked
at each other, the mothers and fathers,
the younger siblings who woke up alive.
not a single person knew how to grieve
without contrast to quiet their hearts.
usually there is someone not grieving,
someone not weeping to help keep
the food made and the garbage taken out.
but here there was no one. all living
ceased, everyone died. no cooking, no
cleaning, no living of lives, a whole nation
dead, just weeping and wailing
and gnashing of teeth, thousands at once
and everything stopped. egypt crumbled,
closed her shutters, lay in her
bed and didn't get up. that's how
israel walked out untouched for those
first few days. no one in egypt could find
any way to care. nothing mattered anymore,
perhaps it wouldn't ever again.

Fourteen Weeks

at the top of the hill, I made a joke—
"I possess the power of two souls!"
so shortly and so soon my second soul
will leave me, my great mystery,
my freshwater pearl tucked in the
gray clamshell of my body. you are
purely possible. you don't know the world,
and nothing has harmed you. but your
soul is full and weighty. your soul holds
all it ever will. you are behemoth, you
are leviathan, you are mythical monster,
black hole sucking in all density,
white whale lurking under the ship.
I imagine you as a crouching tiger,
hungry for both breakfast and living.
you might devour me whole.

The Red Sea

to walk through on dry land,
though the waves could so easily
come crashing back down on me.
to pass through without cesarean scar,
without panic or emergency,
hemorrhage or baby-can't-breathe.
walking through with firm steps, as if it isn't a miracle.
I will this. I hope this. but I know
I won't know anything until I'm right
in the middle, standing in the space
the sea made. the waters will part,
impossible and red, thick walls of muscle,
the placenta a solid mass. did you know
the body grows a whole new organ in
a matter of weeks, and we hardly talk about it?
will I walk through without being swept away?
through this strange narrow place,
livestock driving full carts piled with furniture,
the dripping walls, the sound of the water loud,
bumping over coral and stone, everything groaning,
being cut or stretched or torn?

but afterward, afterward, the questions can't float.
tell me, will I find myself safe on the other side,
bound for the promised land?
or will I be a shipwrecked chariot,
a tragic woman lost forever to the undertow of her children?
stuck in the broken waters, the passage between?
is this where I drown, in this sea?

Fifteen Weeks

how each trimester spans a
full season. the first in spring,
lying in bed in the dark of a
daylong rain. the second in
summer, sunburned ankles
and sweat, the third in fall,
where I'll become more pumpkin-like
with each passing day, quickening
like leaves kicking up in the wind.
and you'll be winter, the freeze
then thaw, the glow of a candle,
the icy street at dawn.

I stopped being able to pray

I stopped being able to pray—except
for the prayer of my body building a body,
adding liters of blood to my veins.

I stopped knowing at all what to say—except
help and why and where and when,
each single-worded question quick to my lips.

      I lost what I had, felt my mind become quiet.
      time stepped over me, walked away,
      while I sat, twisted, on the couch.

I stopped being able to pray—instead,
I watched from windows, walked the dog,
washed the dishes, felt thoughts intrude,

      and wept, over and over. what else could I do?
      as if the weeping would build this baby too.

Fifteen and a Half Weeks

oddly, no one really asks me how I feel.
if they did, I'd have a thousand answers.
I feel like a wave rushing toward breaking.
like an arrow being pulled back in a bow.
like a bell before its ringing, like a ripening
apple, like a foghorn surrounded by sun.
I feel antsy and hopeful, worn out and worried.
who is more real, my baby or me?
I wait like a windchime for the wind.

Rebekah

she holds their identical
heads in her palms, a body
against each forearm.
esau wiggles and cries,
has his own life to make,
almost falls down to the floor.
but jacob, magic one,
holds a lock of her hair
in his hand, eyes gazing,
like she and him are
the same, looking in a
strange mirror, she sees
her soul in his face,

and something in her
splits in two. she never
meant for it to happen,
will never be able to forget

the secret curse, secret
blessing, favorite son.

Sixteen Weeks

time has slowed to a stop,
and I've hardly gotten rounder.

the weeks feel interminable,
and each one has a number.
I've never kept time in weeks before.

the days are hot, and sometimes it rains.
I can't do anything quickly, not even grow a baby.
I feel like I can't do anything at all.

Leah

birth after birth after birth
and still no sign that it has
changed anything at all. I have
only my babies for comfort,
only one talent. my womb's his
wife, not me. with each new
child I think, *this is the one*.
each strong boy I bear just
stacks atop the rest, everything
blurry except them. I think
they're the best children in
this terrible world. I think what
I've done is good.

Seventeen Weeks

by the fire, my mom and missy sit and
talk about their late miscarriages,
one at sixteen weeks, one at twenty-four. they recall
them with a matter-of-factness.
don't worry, my mom says.
that won't be you, it won't be you.
you're already past where I was.
I feel the skin over my uterus pulled taut.
you're growing in there, I'm sure, I hope,
and somehow I'm not afraid. we talk with
a kind of settled wonder, the way of women
to let the mysteries stay unsolved. and
there's a reverence in me, mixed with
a growing fierceness. mine and yours both.
if you die, I will go on living, holding your
perfect possibility in my fist. if you go on living,
I will die in a thousand tiny ways, having met you
on earth where we don't know anything.

Rachel

cold-limbed, like my fingers are frozen.
there must be something I've done wrong,
some terrible sin or mistake I've never
repented. each month I hold my breath

and bleed again. isn't this a sacrifice?
am I now not an altar myself?

cruel dreams where I'm pregnant, then
I wake again to my body's solitude.
I can still imagine a future, but it's
melting as quickly as I freeze,

blowing away like dust from my
dryness, eggs boiling in the

hot water of my desire.
I must have wanted too much.

Eighteen Weeks

I think that life can be good,
though sometimes it's hard to tell.
I sit in the same spot on the couch
every morning with the dog curled
on the other side. I drink one cup
of coffee. I look at the tree. Later,
I walk the same circular route,
tugging the dog past the herd of deer.
I choose something to wear
and put it on. I cook a small lunch
and eat it on a stool in the corner of
the kitchen. I take up very little space,
I make very little noise. Maybe I will
listen to some music, maybe I will
read a book. In all this you will join me.
All this, you will disrupt. All I have I
will give to you, and what will it add
up to? Something small and big at once.
Though sometimes it's hard to tell,
I think that life can be good.

Dinah

ask me about violence,
ask me about men.
I will say nothing.

ask me about justice,
it's something I don't know.
ask me about mercy,
it's thin, it's harsh.

ask me about lovers,
ask me about time,
the way it piles, heavy,
like layers of wool.

ask me about smallness,
about gardens, about music,

ask me how I feel
when I stand near the sea.

Nineteen Weeks

when I feel you move, it's like a
bubble popping, like the flick of a
wrist, like a fish brushing against
seaweed along the ocean floor. I am
your cosmos, your mountains and trees.
I imagine you exploring, running though
there's no room to run. I imagine you
at home in the garden of me. to you,
I am everything, as far as the eye can
see. the farthest tree, the bird gliding
across the sky. I am strange sounds,
warm water, sugar rush. caffeine in the
morning, the first music you hear.
I won't be your home forever, but right
now I am. a small first earth to live in.
I give that to you.

Rahab

I tie a red ribbon to the window frame.

I take a risk that feels foolish.

Yes, come over for dinner.

I send postcards in a swing state.

I can't protect anyone.

I say things I regret.

I ask him to hold my hand when he comes to bed.

Yes, come hide in my basement.

I don't sleep very well.

I own a really big basket.

I've never been a mother.

I am mostly home alone.

I neglect the garden.

I worry over every choice.

I am scared of snakes.

I wish my friends lived closer.

Yes, I'll hold your baby.

Yes, I'm still hopeful.

Yes, I'm still young.

Yes, I am terrified.

Twenty Weeks

each part of you has been measured,
circumferenced, and transversed. I
lay on the chair and watch you move
on the screen, feeling the strange jabs
from within in agreement. you, sideways,
folded in half, moving your arms and
legs, a hand with visible knuckles, your
mind inside a new skull. like deep sea
diving, like space travel, I see with god-
eyes a place that isn't a place, somewhere
soft, warm, dark. cool summer morning,
sixty-five degrees, and you are heartbeat,
all four chambers. you are open mouth,
blackness marking fluid. you are stomach
and kidneys, and each tiny bone of the spine.
she says you are healthy, you are growing,
you have everything you need. we sit
holding hands, not sure what we are seeing.
you, our own son, alive in your body.
we stop for coffee after, then go home and
let the dog out of the crate. a boy, we say.
a boy. I think of you all day, having finally
seen the hidden shape of your face.

Gomer

I myself am your metaphor, holding your children
at my breast with their names that say
things I don't want to hear.

no mercy, not my people, I carry them,
I wash their skin, I feed them, look into their eyes,
and they are children, not some curse, not some

strange prophecy. I'll be the curse.
I'll be the prophecy. lay their skin on my skin,
and I'll keep them warm with my body's contradictions,

with the lack of mercy, with the homelessness,
put those on me. I'll be *no mercy*. I'll be *not my people*.
I'll be *jezreel*. call them my name

instead. *gomer*, meaning complete.
gomer, meaning whole. or give them
secret nicknames like flower or blue bird. like

juniper. like amethyst. I can be
whatever strange story you need me to be, but
I will give my children names that keep them alive.

Twenty-One Weeks

evening walks through
queen anne's lace season,
city stairways lined with tall pokeweed,
under streetlights, up and down
hills, me slower with hands on hips,
plodding steps. this isn't bliss.
we walk our despair. did you know
the world is terrifying? did you know
the neighborhood's alleys were this narrow
and lined with abandoned televisions
and piles of tires? and beautiful,
did you know it was also this
beautiful and this romantic
in the humid air with mist and cats
hiding under parked cars?
someone's garden is full of
sunflowers, and I will never be
pregnant for the first time again.
once you're born, we'll give you
a place to live, and it's this place.
I show you first in me.

Naomi

where is my mother?
who will mother me?
am I walking forward
alone from this place?

call me mara. call me
sorrow. call me
earthworm. for the
almighty has withheld

goodness. what is safety?
how would it feel
to be held?

Twenty-Two Weeks

have I gotten too caught up in your poetry,
have I not set foot yet on solid enough ground?

you will be human, not poem. you won't be written.
you will astound me with your flesh and my blood.

you'll show up on my doorstep. I remind myself you're real.
kicks like little missives, remembrances of you.

when I think of birth I often think of this:
let it be to me according—
and then the rest trails off. I can't

muster the awareness of god.
I can hardly muster the awareness of you.
maybe both at once. maybe one and the same.

Ruth

have I been desperate?
here is my body
given on the threshing floor—
I'll go wherever you go.
you found me in your fields,
among the barley,
between tall grasses.
I was the clouds,
the soil, the grain.
I don't know if
this is love.
it's thinner,
more like hope.
harvest me.
I'll be ground into
your flour, baked
into your loaves.
if I uncover your feet
and lie down, then
what will you do to me?

Twenty-Three Weeks

and listeria in the food, fumes from newly
paved roads,

and toxoplasmosis tracked in by the dog,

and global pandemic, pneumonia, stillbirth,
preeclampsia,

and botulism, water that bounces
back up from the sink,

and falling down the stairs, norovirus,
black mold, dirty towels touching my mouth,

and handwashing dozens of times a day,
and checking locked doors, gas leaks,
faulty wires,

and lead paint, mercury, pfoa,
drinking too much coffee, not enough folate,

and salmonella on the onions,
or undercooked eggs,

and pokeweed, poison ivy, poison hemlock,

and dog poop on my hands after bagging it up,
swimming in toxic blue-green algae blooms,

and microdroplets in the air from the stranger nearby,

and spores in rice, spoiled food,
browning apples, potatoes with sprouts,
the outside of the milk jug,
the kitchen countertop,

and the pillowcase, the sheets,
boil the toothbrush.

and listeria in the food, and

Wisdom

wisdom wakes in the night.
wisdom checks that the stove isn't on,
the locks on the front door and back.
wisdom stares at the ceiling, listens
for the sound that will scare her.
no sound. wisdom sleeps.

wisdom waits. she wonders what else
she will lose. wisdom talks to her friends
about grief, wastes time, writes things
no one will read. wisdom reads on
the couch for an indulgence of hours,
fills her cup with more water, gets
the sweater from the hook.

wisdom walks, avoiding cats so
the dog won't yank hard on the leash.
wisdom waves at the neighbors, feels sad
when the lilacs are gone for the year.
wisdom asks for what she needs though
it's hard to find the words. wisdom weeps,
stays home, wisdom crosses the street.

wisdom reads message boards, then
emails a friend. wisdom piles up books,
wisdom calls her mom. wisdom cooks
eggs, fills the dog's bowl with food.
wisdom wonders about failure,
about the way the world will end.

Twenty-Four Weeks

my leanness, my leanness.
I am divided from myself,
made to sit in the rocking
chair for ten minutes after
taking the laundry downstairs.
each morning I think I'll
do so many things. at day's
end, it feels like I've done
nothing. what do I want?
I want to sit still. I want
to remember how I felt
a year ago. you're getting
bigger every day—I feel
the weight—and I'm
getting smaller, slower,
more dim.

Proverbs 31

I was just trying to survive. trying not to drown
in the flood of living, trying to feed my babies
and keep our house clean and carry the water
and make a little bit of money, never enough,
and when things were finally quiet at the end
of the day sometimes I'd start weeping,
sometimes I'd very slowly eat a piece of fruit,
sometimes I'd stare at the wall until eventually
I fell asleep exhausted, hands deep in the dishes,
lost in thought, and sometimes I'd quietly
steal away from the house, leaving my husband
sitting down, and run, I'd run as fast as I could
run just to feel my body moving and remember
that I'm ongoing, that there is something in
me alive, that all of this adds up to something,
and under all the things I do, there's me inside.

so you can hold my body like it is a vegetable,
cook it into your stew, catalog my actions and
project them on the wall. my mind is hidden
from you. wake me at night, write me into
your book, read me aloud to a room full of men,
and they will decide what is true.

Twenty-Five Weeks

call me mara, for the almighty has
dealt bitterly with me, though only
in my mind. you've already been
acquainted with my anxiety, before
ever seeing my face, before ever
feeling my skin.

are you filled with dread when I am?
how much of what terrifies me will
I pass on to you, what cortisol, what
adrenaline, what fatigue fills us both?
how do I endanger you when I feel afraid?

a soft dream about breastfeeding you,
then I wake to remember to worry.
I'll give you milk but not honey.
something bitter will pass between us
after the colostrum's gold. you go
where I go, wherever that is. I take
you with me, lamb, to the valley.

last week I floated in a warm swimming
pool, and it was almost as if you took me
with you instead to the still waters, to the
restored soul, to the quiet fearlessness
of the womb.

Song of Solomon

husband, we're young, and it's quiet afternoon.
come close and tell me what you think about us.
our bedroom's curtain closed to the light,
and the dog's asleep out on the couch.

husband, remember parking by the lake?
the sound of the frogs? that great clearing's
tall grass? that tent at the top of the bluff,
us both drenched? each bedroom's own
dark quietness?

husband, wake up and touch my back. I still
dream about you, still see you like this.
which do you think, a boy or a girl? tell me,
do you still see me new?

Grandma Irene's Email

of course, I was reminded of your dad's birth.
when he was a few days old, I nearly panicked—
oh, dear, what have we done?

this child has a never dying soul!

as you might guess, that truth
pretty much set the stage for our lives.

Bathsheba

for all you take from me,
there is so much I keep.
you can't have my flowers and trees.
my breathing, my morning tea.
you can have my love, for it
goes ahead of me, like perfume,
like musk, like my own body.
but I am my own. I am not
husband or son. I am not
murder or grief. I am something
past what has happened to me.
I am not angry, I am living.
I have power I don't need,
wealth I don't want, but I'll
use it to show you that
a woman is always alone.

Twenty-Six Weeks

after a day of thick thunderstorms,
our front door warps and won't latch.
and the wooden fence, the garden gate,
are twisting and expanding.
I'm having trouble closing too,
my softwood body's dampness
warping me after too much water
for too long, the dripping on my head
means I can't finish any thought.
rivulets in the basement and a chimney leak.
I am full of unnecessary false-grief,
anxiety's cruel sister, overactive premonitions.
we need to clean our gutters, so the patio flooded.
but now the water's been absorbed.
the only evidence it was there is the way
I have to fling myself against the door
to get it to stay shut. whatever lightness
I'd had, it's gone. I am left ajar.

Annunciation

when did I open my mouth? It hangs ajar.
my soul doth weep and scream—contained
in pinpoint eternity, the knife of this moment, slit.
I'll never leave this room again without being torn in two.
and my spirit doth hang open like an empty bag, the fruit
having all tumbled out when over my shoulder I saw
something out of place—moon and stars in full daylight—
a slant shadow, crack in the floor where I tumbled too.
I am alone. I am undone, divided by euphoria,
sliced by my own unblinking answer to—

I'm sitting in the dirt, my clothes are damp,
I'm sweating, with colors behind my eyelids and terrible
ringing in my ears, and I'll feel this way forever,
how could I not? an apple, bruised,
rolled far under the table, and it's all I can do
not to crawl and retrieve it and put it back,
put all of them back and then crawl
out the door with them—stand up
and run. or leave the apples to rot.

what do I sing? where do I write it down,
why have all the pens gone missing?
when did I open my mouth?

my soul, my soul, my soul doth open wide,
and I don't know any other songs.
I've already forgotten myself, who I've been,
because I'm not anymore. I am newness itself.
this is where I live now, in this body full of fire.
smear the ashes on my forehead, clothe me in
sackcloth, I'll lay on my side, unmoving, until—

I sit still on the floor the rest of the afternoon,
practice breathing, watch the sun disappear,
see a candle flickering on the table,
a candle I don't think I lit.

Twenty-Six and a Half Weeks

I do believe
     I'm beginning to resemble
          the moon.

Mary

1. my son

my son takes my life, makes
it feel like a door closed behind me
and locked, leaves me alone
with newness and the fullness of time.

my son takes my mind, I can't remember
how I used to think, what it used
to feel like to move from one day
to another.

my son takes my body, replaces it
with something softer and more useful,
more connected to skin
and the earth, the tide and moon,
leaving me weeping at the curves
of the hills I grew up on.

my son takes my soul, changes what it
means to live, gives me work to do.
at first I think I'm meant to keep him alive,
now I see I'm meant instead
to let him do whatever it is he'll do.
I can imagine a new heaven,
I am in a new earth. he is born,
and I'm born again.

2. our hidden life

you weren't marvelous. you were ordinary.
you ate and pooped and screamed,
were precocious, disagreeable,
couldn't be reasoned with.

it amazed me when you would ask me a
question, so many, and look at me,
waiting for an answer.
as if you didn't know already.
you really didn't know.

I was so prepared for our life to be
strange. but you were a child,
my own dear baby. toward you
I felt a reverence that wasn't unusual
—I'd seen it in other mothers gazing
at other babies whose births weren't
accompanied by angel song.

so we lived a golden hour,
and I forgot your future for a while.
our hidden life, my secret pride.
I think I got the best of you.

3. *a sword will pierce your own soul, too*

that time we lost you,
when you went off alone
in the temple to teach adult men.

I was running, wracking my brain for
some prophecy, some instruction.
I'd had one job, and I'd failed.

how could you scare me?
this terrible feeling?

I felt you pulled from my
side like a spear,

all my waters rushing out.

4. *pieta*

I waited all your life for this,
felt it coming like a panther
stalking us from behind.
a gasp in the middle of the
night, waking from a dream,
this murder hill. I've been
here before in my sleep.

every mother knows their
child will die sometime.

know this, my baby.
I'd die on that cross,
take the cup from you
if it meant you suffered less.

but that isn't what you
need from me. all you
ever needed was for me
to hold you so close
and then let you go

to hell or heaven
or both.

Twenty-Seven Weeks

our first and only language is silence.

all I know of you is you will change and change and change.

she asked if I talk to you much. "no," I said.

but I remember you and think of you
and also, yes, believe in you.

at the baby shower, I wear a dress that makes me
feel like meg ryan in a romantic comedy.

it shows you off, your body inside my body.

when repeatedly asked how I feel, the word I use most is *surreal*.

but really, I have no words.
really, I cannot speak.

later, I'm revising poems, reading out loud
on the couch, and you kick.

can you hear my voice, you hidden burning thing?

Elizabeth

time forgot her, taught her to forget,
so she gave herself to it. more minutes.
more months. more work to do,
more bread to knead and bake and eat
with butter and milk,
more husbands and husbandry.

she wasn't waiting. no,
elizabeth enjoyed her solitude.
a woman can drown in longing,
and she didn't want to drown.
people on the shore saying about her
words like *disgrace*, so much easier not to hear.
so she swam, sure strokes, strong arms
and strong legs, perfect form, kicking,
splashing pearls of water behind her as she went.

miracles set you off-balance.
break your rhythm, add weight.
elizabeth was undone, drowning,
sitting on the sea's floor. such good news
—so why was she weeping all the time?
to fill the ocean with more saltwater?

it wasn't until mary walked up the road,
dusty and round, it wasn't until
she felt her own baby
leap from the waves like
the fish that swallowed jonah,
that elizabeth was able
to come up to the surface,
take one deep, long breath,
floating on her back.
blessed are you among women,
and maybe I'm blessed too.

Twenty-Eight Weeks

in our meeting, she asks me,
"what do you want to remember of this
time?" and I think—*remember?*
I want this time, this year, these last
twelve weeks to run over me like water
and drain away toward the sea.
all of us edge closer and closer
to apocalypse. you, me, and everything.
it's all grown more absurd
with each passing week,
my body's new shapes, fires
all along the west coast,
an incident with a groundhog.
don't say *it can't get worse*, it can.
I expect, with trembling, it will.
you'll be born at some sort of end
of the world. everywhere we go
together will be brand new,
not just for us, but for everyone.

you will be the purest among us,
most wise, most willing to let
the world be whatever ruin it is,
loving it precisely because it's
all you've known. my body
will be broken, and your body
will be whole, and we'll go out
together to see what remains.

Magnificat

my soul magnifies something small in me,
and my spirit rejoices in what suddenly feels like hope.

I am being regarded, and
all generations will call me blessed.

this isn't gentle, but it's good.
the knife's edge of grief.

and the sort of holiness that's so bright
it's hard to take in with open eyes,

obscured by skin, by body, ordinary time.

maybe there is mercy in the fear of god,
in knowing how delicate it is to be alive.

could it be that what is happening to me is big?

could it scatter the proud? could it undo the evil?

no. but there's a dream where women and children
are asked what they think. where the lowest ones stand tall,
where the hungry are filled, the rich are emptied.

I will try to say it plainly,
but it will come out as a strange song.

if this is a way we survive,
then let it be whatever it will be.

Twenty-Nine Weeks

a couple loses their dog in the woods
where we're walking, saturday afternoon,
and they ask us to keep an eye out.
I see my husband silently resolve
to find him. white pitbull in a blue shirt,
must have run off following a squirrel
and found himself alone and further
than he thought. we call his name, "cash!"
scanning the trees which seem
even more quiet than usual,
almost no movement at all. it seems
impossible that anything here could
be out of place, impossible that we'd
spot him. down toward the ravine
and the creek the air gets cooler, more
moss, more dampness, Isaiah's ahead
on the trail, and I hear his voice change.
"did you find him?" he calls back, "yes!"
no surprise, he knew where to look,
and sure enough, cash is here and nervous,
too good at dodging for us to grab his collar,
tail between his legs, and, yes, the blue shirt,
sweet face, soft eyes. our own dog befriends
him, they play with a ball until he runs away
from us, this time in the right direction.
Isaiah pursues with our dog, proud and
rushing after cash in the blue shirt, making
sure he doesn't lose sight of him again,
                                    and then,
I am alone, slow and pregnant in the ravine,
not a lost dog, just left to climb up by myself.

Visitation

there's a way among some women
to join you where you are,
come running down the road
when they see you approaching,
rushing past the mailbox
to meet you halfway.
you don't even need to make it far enough
to have to knock on the door.
they were waiting at the window for you.

Thirty Weeks

there's a comfort in the soft things
I'm gathering for you. finally
something physical to touch.
I started knitting you some socks,
sat on the couch for afternoon hours
adding stitches to your quilt.
I want to cover you in wool,
more sweaters, more hats.
your clothes that will hold you,
empty but cheerful, are a glimpse
at your body's dimensions.
I conjure the weight of you,
your warmth in my arms,
folding small pants thinking
about how they will cover
your own small legs.
I want you revealed,
I want you cloth diapered,
wrapped in muslin, little socks.
now you are metaphysical,
but not for too long.
soon, body. soon, breath.
soon, clothed in the cotton I gather,
sleeping on crib sheets I so carefully chose,
a sheepskin in a moses basket,
a secondhand bassinet, something
called a *lounger*, a wood rocking chair
covered in blue plush cushions.
all of this I gather around me
as if it will bring you forth.

I become softer in turn, less tough.
no way to steel myself against loss anymore,
with so many tiny onesies
waiting so quietly to be worn.

Virginity

have I been recollected yet?

in pregnancy's new virginity,
my body restores its innocence.
everything wonder, everything
strange, and there is something
pure in my waiting.

my skin, my hair, my teeth.

you'd think it the opposite,
but here something is given
instead of taken away. what
thrills me most is how ordinary
it feels for my body to change

so easily and so completely.

Thirty-One Weeks

I find new eschatology in you,
your body making mine new
and old. strange apocalypse
mirrored by creation from
nothing, a big bang of cells
that now kicks and flips in me.
the world is more wild now
than I've ever seen it before.
we are hurtling through prophecies,
a news cycle of minutes
rather than hours or days or weeks.
alas for women who are pregnant
and for those who are nursing
infants in those days. how can
I absorb this world while trying
to build one more tender than
I've known? I can't. I won't.
I become a sort of center,
conjuring the eye of the hurricane,
living instead in some future
that is safe, imagining heaven
like it's the home I sleep in,
tossing and turning but
still alive when morning breaks.
what will be the end of my world?
what will be the beginning of yours?

Jesus

will you stay awake with me
or wake up for the first time?
will you stay here in the garden
and weep with me and I with
you? the night is far spent, and
soon it will be day. we are nearer
than we have ever been to
knowing what is true.

will you sit with me in the dim
half light, the moon through the
window, the rocking chair? will you
listen while I cry about how it feels
to live? will you hold me very gently,
no matter how long or how late?

I don't mean to speak in riddles, I just
don't know what will happen.
there is a faint glimmer, a memory
I have, something about the weather
and the smell on the edge of the wind.
it's getting cold, I need you here.
will you stay awake with me?

Thirty-Two Weeks

I begin to imagine you real.
one who will eat every two hours,
one who will wake me up,
steal not just my sleep but
my life out from under me.
I begin to imagine you
legs and arms, covered in
vernix, wait to wash you
so the moisture can soak in.
I begin to imagine your
fingernails, how we'll have
to figure out how to file them
without harming your skin,
your bird mouth and the
shapes you will take.
I begin to imagine you
christmas, with music.
I begin to imagine you
kitchen in a carrier
or swaddled and laid flat
on your back in a bassinet.
I imagine you safe,
I imagine you sick,
I imagine you terrifying
and comforting, both.
I imagine myself,
someone new after you.
Who is she, your mother?

The Bleeding Woman

I could touch you so gently that you wouldn't even feel it.
I could speak so quietly, use only vowels,
I could be so small, be your mustard seed,
little potato bug, little smear of blood on a
clean white cloth, I could scrub that,
I could wash all your clothes,
your hem in my hand,
touch you so softly that you
wouldn't mind my reaching out
so small, so little, just my index finger,
just a pincer grasp, just the edge of you,
I could fit into your pocket, write my
address on a napkin, little envelope scrap,
tell you a sad story you'd forget instantly,
I could dance so quietly in the corner of the room,
and you wouldn't even see me,
you wouldn't even know.

Thirty-Three Weeks

a growing anger in me like
heavy clouds, october's earlier
darkness. what do I call this
suffering? what name for it?

we walk and argue. he's
angry too. where we both
need a circle of gentleness,
angles and corners instead.

the dog stops to press his nose
to the sidewalk, and we both
stand and wait. two people,
silent, triangulated by love.

I walk a few paces behind
until later I'm tearful and
walking ahead, plodding
forward as if it gives me power.

he touches every tree. he
breaks dead branches, bends
stems. he does things that
startle me without realizing.

the questions I ask go
unanswered. the demands
I make feel thin. I don't present
a good case. too exhausted.

be careful not to trip,
he says. *the uneven sidewalk,
the cracks.* we do not touch.
we do not hold hands.

even still, I'd rather walk
together than stay home alone
in the growing darkness,
silent house, under skies full of clouds.

The Syrophoenecian Woman

yes lord, but even the dogs, even the dogs
get the scraps of food. yes lord, is my child
a dog, am I a dog to you? yes lord, what will
you say to a person standing in front of you
asking for help? yes lord, I'm a mother
whose child is suffering, a mother who
is suffering as her child suffers. I am a
squeaky wheel, a leaky faucet, I am a dog,
and I won't stop barking. I am tireless,
I am fearful, I am here in front of you.

yes lord, the welfare check, the daycare bill,
the health insurance. yes lord, the alimony,
the unemployment, the bank account,
the fear of god. yes lord, the lump in my breast,
the landlord, the want ad, the terrified.

yes lord, but even the dogs.
heal my daughter.
do it.

Thirty-Four Weeks

you'll be politics, you'll be pandemic.
you'll be climate, health care, taxes.
you will take the world we hand to you,
your hands learning how to grasp.
I welcome your perspective,
new-eyed and blinking america.

I voted for a president
on behalf of you.

I've absorbed what I could,
tried to remain calm
so your waters could be settled,
perhaps for the last time.
this world is not gentle.
this country is not good.
you will be a citizen—
I can't even tell you
what that means.

Mary and Martha

let me sit.
let me work.
I need to be close to you.
I need to make something happen,
take some sort of control.
I need quiet.
I need music.
everything can wait.
so much needs to happen.
there's no time.
there's no time.
time doesn't mean anything.
I am stuck in time.
underwater.
earth.
hearth.
dishwasher.
I'd crawl into your skin if I could.
you don't understand what it's like.
I am your guest.
I am your host.
there is nothing I need.
are you hungry?
I'm so hungry.
my name is your name.
say my name.
please say my name.
if only you were here when I needed you.
running toward you,
kicking up the dust on the road
making more laundry to do.

Thirty-Five Weeks

standing just outside the trader joe's checkout line,
absent-faced, holding a tube of hand lotion.
where am I? what am I doing?

haven't been walking.
spending too much on groceries.
failing at "eating well."
mostly well hydrated.
anxious, anxious, anxious.

feeling very outside myself.
foreign body.
who am I? where am I going?

existential confusion.
body in a strange state of uncomfortable homeostasis.
the alien feeling of something moving from the inside.

I'm worried I'm losing my husband somehow,
betraying him by changing. also by wanting him
to change with me, grow nearer.
maybe he is?

do I betray myself by changing?
what good thing will happen?

are you ready? the cashier asks me,
my face is white and long,
looking always like I've just seen a ghost.

The Woman Caught in Adultery

I have valued honesty. Just look at me before you
kill me. Before you think of killing me. Before you
choose a stone from the pile of stones, before you
hold that stone in your hand, touch that stone's
hard skin, ask it to sing some sort of worship song,
impossibly. I will tell you the truth, answer all
of your questions. Have you been beyond reproach?
I will die if you kill me. I would make a great wife.
I've had a life, and it has been mine. No man has
ever known what I was thinking. I will work until sunrise,
I will walk anywhere. I'm not sure when the possibilities
began to drain away. I looked up, and they had all gone.

Thirty-Six Weeks

I have cherished my solitude,
my quiet hours walking circles
in the house without you.

I will cherish you too
but differently.

The Woman at the Well

I'm thirsty. I thirst, and I always have. with every
friend and lover, something they can't give me, some
part of me they can't touch. I come here every day
to draw water, to feel my feet hit the earth, to think,
and each day I drink and must return, it never ends,
I haven't been satisfied.

what is my life, though, without this well? without
the wanting, the waking at night parched? who am I
without desire, without the touch of a new stranger,
the steady understanding that everyone leaves?
if I stop being thirsty, what keeps going in me?
can you answer that question, man with bright dark eyes?

Thirty-Seven Weeks

what desire, what dread?
you've grown too heavy
in my body. I cannot remember
anymore the weightlessness
of carrying only myself.
has this all only been prologue?
what will you write into me?

each day I wake up and wonder,
today? last week's ultrasound
to see your hand draped across
your forehead, the same position
I take when distressed, pressing
my fingers into my eyes. already
you've known me too intimately,
hearing the blood in my veins,
breathing the fluid I made.

doubled laundry, exhaustion,
split mind. I am divided by you.
even now, I wake up a dozen times
in the night, as if you're already
here crying out. I labor to turn over
in the damp quiet. I go back to sleep.

there is no returning. there is
no regret, only quietness that
presses and pulls at my mind.
I'm at the point now where
pregnancy's worn thin, not
warm enough against the wind.
I'd like to be your mother.
I'd like to ruin my life.

Alabaster Jar

I'll clean
your feet
with my
tears and
my hair.
I'll go
too far,
I'll say
too much.
I'll open
the most
precious thing
I have
and pour
it all
over you
in front
of everyone,
every day
for the
rest of
my life.

Thirty-Eight Weeks

but today the table is a wilderness
of objects, and it has been for weeks.
I flinch to look over, feel a strange
wash of shame. yes, there are the brass
candlesticks with pink tapers,
the dried flowers in a striped vase,
the coasters decorated with cartoon
maitre d's, the bouquet my friend sent
from minnesota after I cried on the
phone. this table could be beautiful.
this table could be neat, finely set
with cloth napkins, surrounded by friends
or used for dinner even only by me
and my husband, sitting quietly
in the early darkness, our forks
chiming against porcelain plates.
instead, the table only reflects my chaos,
the swirling sense that something is
undone. piles of mail, empty water jug,
laundry folded and not put away.
a plastic tub of wool diaper covers
that need to be washed gently in lavender
and slathered in lanolin to become
waterproof. a layer of dust gains
height each day. it could all be beautiful,
like a still life, oil-painted portrait
of these isolating days. the table framed
by wide windows, the floor swept clean.
my fear has found a resting place, the
table's flat expanse. if I cleared it off,
how would that feel? I have nothing to say.

Daughters of Jerusalem

the days have come when they will say aloud
blessed are the barren, those without children,
the empty wombs, the breasts that have never nursed.
blessed are the light-footed, the ones with less to lose.
and who is that? who hasn't wanted all there is?
the mountains are falling, the hills will cover everything.
the wood is still green, but how long until it's dry?

a sword will pierce your heart too,
though you hope it will pass you by.
innocent with your hopefulness,
daughters of jerusalem, don't weep for me,
but weep for yourselves and, even more,
for your children. for the earth you give them,
your own weakness, the fact that you will die
and can't shelter them forever, that you
can't even protect yourself.

what will you do when the end comes?
find yourself at the bottom of everything,
always at the threshold of the door you fear most.
you will each know this sorrow, feel split in two,
watch your own bloody heart be laid in the tomb.

The Earth

the earth, a mother, imagines hundreds of ways
her children could die, sees it happen in her dreams
over and over, feels their blood seep into her skin,
their bodies buried in her soil, wanders hospital
halls desperately, their cells still moving through
her body long after birth. the earth conjures disasters,
earthquakes, fires, terrible magical thinking
in the darkness of night.

the mistake was having children. the earth without
people would have flourished with verdant green.
less to love, more space to spread out.
but she ached for them, dreamed of them,
asked for them until they came. and they undid her,
little by little, used her every part, warmed her past heat,
killed her so slowly, with fear, with ambition,
with love.

Thirty-Nine Weeks

I'm singing a song called
when will my baby be born?—
hesitant, melodic, good
for bouncing on a big
purple ball in the bedroom,
phantom contractions all
day long that are false labor.
I am both relieved and disappointed.

I'm singing a song called
what do I do with myself?
telling Isaiah, "I don't want
to create or produce anything,"
and if not, then what shall I
set my hands to? even this
poem is too much to make.
I feel weepy at the window.
my last glimpses of this world.

Mary at the Tomb

that nightmare where your beloved is dead
that nightmare where your beloved is
dead that
nightmare where
your beloved is
dead.

that world that doesn't have him
that half-world that isn't good anymore
half-good
that nightmare

where
there's a tomb
and he's in it

where
there's a tomb
and he's not in it

that nightmare where your beloved is dead
and missing dead and missing

and missing
missing

and

where have you taken him?

The Woman with the Stars on her Head

and there appeared a great wonder,
a woman clothed with the sun,
and the moon under her feet,
and a crown of twelve stars on her head,
pregnant, in labor, deep moans of birth,
somewhere between living and dead,

and there appeared another wonder,
a great red dragon, with
seven heads and ten horns,
and seven crowns on his heads,
standing over the woman, waiting
to eat her baby as soon as it was born.

she gave birth to a boy who was
whisked away to heaven. she didn't
see what happened, too quick for her to know.
desperate, running to the wilderness, to see
if her baby was there, she found a place to hide
for one thousand, two hundred, and sixty days,
too many days to search and wait.

meanwhile, a war in heaven.
meanwhile, a war in her.
the dragon sent to earth,
the woman sent to, what?

the woman was given two wings like an eagle
so she could always fly back to her place. to wait longer,
for a time and times and half a time.
how many days is that?

she used the wings to fly across the whole earth,
to scan the landscape for her child,
to find where he had gone. each day
a new flight, new places to look,
dodging the dragon, who wanted her dead.

where was her son? where was her son?
dragons were nothing, but where was her son?

the dragon tried to drown her.
she wanted to be drowned.
the earth wouldn't let her, it bore her up.
she couldn't help but float,
couldn't be heavy enough.

so the dragon grew tired of trying to kill her,
and she grew tired of flying around.
left alone at home wearing the cosmos,
wings hanging limply from a hook on the wall,

nowhere left to look,
nothing left to fight.

End Times

these are end times.
dare I admit now that a poet
expecting a baby fears
the loss of her mind?
I shudder at the premonition
of three wise men visiting
to lay at my feet,
as I hold my small son,
things I cannot figure out how to use.

please leave us alone here in this stable,
my blood and waters intermingled with hay,
vernix-covered infant in a trough,
my body half-naked and grotesque.

leave us, you shepherds,
you village folk, you angels.

let me see the baby first, alone.
we'll sort this out with time.

Labor

you can't remember pain. you inhabit it
like a tent pitched quickly in the rain,
try to survive the night, then in the morning,
you leave that place behind, never to return.

I remember thinking, very clearly,
"I will never do this again." now,
with fear and trembling, I hope or
know I will. but that labyrinthine

walk, my trembling arms and legs,
the wild sensation of my water breaking
in that disco-lit bathtub, and the full moon
I gazed at when I paused for a contraction,

walking to the car. strange forward
momentum, the feeling I may die inside,
the night's terrible plod toward morning.
no deep breathing could deliver me,

I realized they all lied. the only way out
is through and through and underneath
until you're bleeding at the bottom
of the well looking up. why on earth

would I return?
and how could I not?

Revelations

you'd never like earth if you didn't like heaven,
and I don't know if hell exists.
do you like gemstones? trees? coral?

don't worry, just remember you
will live first and then die, return
to something, somewhere,

newness of time,
without end,
a sea-change.

we'll meet for the first time.
both of us no-age, both of us
the same age at once.

but more important,
you'll get to go back to where you came from,
unlatching eden's gates.

I promise you'll remember when you're there—
but it will be different, your eyes having
seen earth and loved it—

coming back to taller grasses
and the oldest,
most constant landscape.

Birth

1.

I've been inside the mystery
and lived. circled the city
seven times with trumpets
until the walls tumbled overhead.

a whale swallowed me, and
I was alive inside a while. and
the red sea? its waves pummeled
my body, a great wall of
water falling straight down
and down and down.
I was a bush, burning.

I saw its back, the mystery.
had I seen its front, I would
have died. the ground was like
sapphires under my feet.

the water in the bathtub glittered
with noah's wife's rainbow until my
water broke. please don't flood
my beloved earth again.

does my face shine like moses's did?
will you read these commandments
scrawled on my stone tablets?

during contractions, in the shower,
I remembered dancing. I pointed
my toes, lifted up to relevé. there
was some strange miraculous relief.

who will ascend god's holy mountain?
where does my help come from?
is the only answer dancing? is
pure survival the truest prayer?

after the episiotomy, he was born,
and I shrieked, then laughed and
laughed. like sarah tucked behind
the mystery's veil as it tore in two,
revealing her impossible son.

2.

tuesday, sex in the afternoon, didn't think it worked,
but then growing but irregular contractions all night,
up at two in pain, watched *While You Were Sleeping*,
layed on the couch, light sleep, ate corn flakes.
didn't wake Isaiah up.

wednesday, due date, in labor all day, hopeful,
called the midwife, bloody show, took a picture on my phone,
midwife check in the afternoon, 4 cm, 80% effaced,
she said "I think you'll be back tonight."
calm steady labor till evening, called the midwife again,
shift change, ate two slices of pizza, same song over and over.
contractions still irregular, getting more painful,
watched *Two Weeks Notice*, contractions 2.5 min apart,
went to the birth center at 11 something, full moon,
hated being in the car, every bump, every bump,
so many roads made of brick. kara midwife, carly nurse,
checked, 4 cm, 100% effaced, midnight.

thursday, intense labor at the birth center, quiet and afraid,
bed, chair, uncontrollable trembling in my arms and legs,
baby's heart rate fine,
alone in the shower for a long time,
fantasized about epidurals and having
no more babies ever again,
Isaiah very tired and very calm,
tub felt good, water broke underwater,
strangest sensation,
out, terrible terrible transition (wasn't sure),
nitrous oxide not helping,
urge to push, oh no (4:11 am),
two women at the birth center delivering at once.
chaos, midwife called in backup,
people talking around and over me,
entering and leaving the room.
I am aware and unaware.
I don't feel afraid,
long time pushing,
long, long time,
midwife theresa comes,
crowning, ring of fire, felt his head,
heart rate drop, episiotomy,
scream, born 5:37 am

Eve, ii

I don't think I can comfort you.

nothing comforted me.

the first death was my child.

the first mistake was my own.

I was in eden, and I left.

but I held my babies in the
world when it was new,

and it felt so much the same.
it felt eternal.

that's something.

think of that.

Thomas

showering a few days after your birth,
I notice blood, yours and mine, under
my fingernails. I wash it down the drain.

thomas puts his hand into the wound
in christ's side, touches that inside
place, unbelievable proof

that something was torn open, something
was born. christ's blood under his
fingernails for the rest of his life.

we name you thomas, call you holy
doubter, lord I believe, help
thou my unbelief, and this child

who broke my body and
appeared here in my arms.

Acknowledgments

"Ash Wednesday" in *The Windhover*
"Eve" in *Image Journal*
"End Times" in *Ekstasis Magazine*
"Revelations" in *Windfall Room*

Title Index

V

W

First Line Index